BRAZIL

by Joanna J. Robinson

The Child's World®

Published by The Child's World®
1980 Lookout Drive • Mankato, MN 56003-1705
800-599-READ • www.childsworld.com

Acknowledgments
The Child's World®: Mary Berendes, Publishing Director
Red Line Editorial: Editorial direction
The Design Lab: Design
Amnet: Production

Design elements: Shutterstock Images; Asaf Eliason/Shutterstock Images
Photographs ©: Shutterstock Images, cover (left top), cover (left bottom),
1 (top), 1 (bottom right), 18 (right), 23, 28; Asaf Eliason/Shutterstock
Images, cover (left center), 1 (bottom left), 18 (left); Andrew Rich/
iStockphoto, cover (right), 24; Christian Wilkinson/Shutterstock Images,
5; Anton Ivanov/Shutterstock Images, 6-7; iStockphoto, 8, 10, 11,
12, 17, 20, 21, 25, 29 30; Stephen Meese/iStockphoto, 13; Jose
Moraes/iStockphoto, 14; Peeter Viisimaa/iStockphoto, 16; Tero
Hakala/Shutterstock Images, 26; Filipe Frazao/Shutterstock Images, 27

ISBN 9781634070386
LCCN 2014959741

Printed in the United States of America
Mankato, MN
July, 2015
PA02268

ABOUT THE AUTHOR

Joanna J. Robinson is a creative educational writer. She has a passion for providing fun learning materials for children of all ages. Robinson has written educational content and more than 100 original stories. Trips to Mexico, Italy, England, Canada, and Egypt inspire Robinson to share her experiences with young readers.

ONE WORLD • MANY COUNTRIES

TABLE OF CONTENTS

ARCTIC
OCEAN

ATLANTIC
OCEAN

PACIFIC
OCEAN

PACIFIC
OCEAN

BRAZIL

INDIAN
OCEAN

SCALE

0   1000 Miles

0   1000 KM

N
W   E
S

SOUTHERN
OCEAN

FUN FACT

ONE WORLD · MANY COUNTRIES

Brazil means "red like an ember." The Brazilwood tree once grew along the coast. It produced a deep, red dye.

CHAPTER 1

WELCOME TO BRAZIL!

Rain pours down. A spider monkey swings between trees, looking for shelter. Jaguars and cougars are already taking cover. Steam hovers in the air as the rain cools the earth.

Life in the Amazon is filled with wild creatures and adventure.

Children run barefoot in the rain. The weather does not interrupt their game of hide and seek. Girls chase monkeys. Boys swim in the river. They pick fresh guava or bananas for a snack.

In many ways, village life here has changed little in hundreds of years. Men teach children how to fish. Boys hunt for turtles, birds, capybara, and caiman.

Women garden, cook, and harvest wild rice. Girls collect nuts, fruits, and seeds. Children learn which plants are useful as medicine or food.

Amazon tribes respect the rain forest. It covers more than half of Brazil.

Thirty million people live in this area.

Protecting the Amazon rain forest is a global issue. Its trees produce 20 percent of Earth's oxygen. Groups from around the world try to protect the rain forest's animals, stop pollution, and prevent **deforestation**. People from all over the world want to see Brazil and its rain forest have a bright future.

A woman from the Amazon travels on a river by wooden boat.

CHAPTER 2

THE LAND

Brazil's coastline is 4,655 miles (7,491 km) long.

Brazil is in South America. It is a large country. Brazil covers about half of South America. Brazil borders every country in South America except for Chile and Ecuador. The Atlantic Ocean forms Brazil's eastern border.

Brazil's best-known feature is the Amazon rain forest. It is in northern Brazil. The rain forest is home to Earth's greatest

The Amazon River is the longest river in South America. It flows for approximately 4,000 miles (6,400 km).

variety of plants. More than 40,000 plants grow there. The tallest trees of the rain forest form a canopy. Plants below the canopy are called the **understory**. The understory is dark. Little sunlight reaches the ground. Mosses and ferns grow there.

A great variety of animals live in the rain forest, too. About 430 kinds of mammals live there. They include monkeys, jaguars, and tapirs. Bats and rodents make up the largest number of animals in the rain forest. Many kinds of frogs, snakes, and insects live there, too.

A mighty river flows through the Amazon **basin**. It is the Amazon River. It enters Brazil along its border with Peru. The river then flows across northern Brazil. Along its path are wild, thick jungles. The river then empties into the Atlantic Ocean.

Outside of the Amazon basin, the land is different. Highlands make up about half of Brazil's land. They cover parts of central, eastern, and southern Brazil. The highlands have rolling hills, flat plains, and steep cliffs.

A cowboy herds cattle on the plains near São Paulo.

The Iguaçu Falls stretch for 1.7 miles (2.7 km).

The cliffs near Argentina's border have a large waterfall. It is Iguaçu Falls. Water from the Iguaçu River drops down a cliff shaped like a horseshoe. Mist from the falling water creates many rainbows.

The land along Brazil's Atlantic coast is flat. It has swamps, sand dunes, and rocky areas. The coast is also famous for its white sand beaches. Many of the beaches are protected by coral reefs. The reefs prevent large waves and storms from destroying the beaches.

Brazil's regions have different climates. On the coast, the climate is warm. The highlands have mild temperatures. The northeast is dry. Across Brazil, temperatures average between 70 and 80 degrees Fahrenheit (21°C and 27°C).

Brazil's land is its best resource. Rich soil is good for growing crops. Brazil is the world's largest coffee grower. It also grows one-third of the world's oranges. Its grassy plains are good for **livestock**, such as cattle. Brazil has one of the world's largest livestock populations.

The Amazon rain forest is home to the world's largest rodent, the capybara. It can grow to be 4 feet (1.2 m) long and weigh up to 145 pounds (66 kg).

FUN FACT

ONE WORLD · MANY COUNTRIES

CHAPTER 3

GOVERNMENT AND CITIES

Brazil's official name is the Federative **Republic** of Brazil. Its citizens elect the president. The president is the chief of state and head of government. Citizens also elect lawmakers. They are called the National Congress.

Brazil's lawmakers meet in the National Congress Building in Brasília.

Rio de Janeiro's beaches are famous for their white sand, blue water, and warm weather.

Brazil has 26 states. The states have local governments. They each have their own leaders, courts, and lawmakers. Brazil also has one federal district. Within the federal district is the nation's capital, Brasília.

Construction of Brasília began in 1956. It is in the center of the country. Brasília was built to replace Rio de Janeiro as the nation's capital. Today, Brasília is known for its modern buildings and city design.

The city of Rio de Janeiro is on the shores of the Atlantic Ocean. Many people enjoy visiting its beautiful beaches. Copacabana Beach and Ipanema Beach are the most famous.

Rio also is known for Corcovado Mountain. People like to climb to the peak. At the top of the mountain is a statue called *Christ the Redeemer*. It is one of Brazil's most famous landmarks.

Brazil's largest city is São Paulo. More than 10.9 million people live there. The city's nickname is Sampa. Sampa is one of the world's fastest growing cities. It is Brazil's center of business.

The *Christ the Redeemer* statue is made of concrete and is 98 feet (30 m) tall. It was completed in 1931.

Brazil's **economy** is growing. Mining, manufacturing, and services are Brazil's biggest industries. Manufacturers make textiles, airplanes, and machines. Farmers also produce many goods. Brazilian coffee and sugarcane are used throughout the world. Goods are **exported** to China, the United States, and Argentina.

Brazil's currency

Brazil's flag

In Portuguese, Rio de Janeiro means "January River." The city received its name from Portuguese explorers on January 1, 1502. They mistakenly thought the city's bay was a river.

FUN FACT · ONE WORLD MANY COUNTRIES

GLOBAL CONNECTIONS

In April 2014, children ages 13 to 17 played in the Street Child World Cup in Rio de Janeiro, Brazil. Children from 19 countries participated.

The goal of this soccer tournament was to raise awareness about street children. Supporters work to protect the children. Sponsors provide scholarships, jobs, and housing. Large companies donate money, too.

Soccer games were just part of the ten-day event. Children and organizers shared ideas about how to help homeless children. They created a Rio Rights Declaration, which was shared with the United Nations.

The event has been successful. Pakistan passed a resolution to protect 1.5 million street children. Brazil started a Children Are Not from the Streets campaign. Many were children reunited with their families.

CHAPTER 4
PEOPLE AND CULTURES

People from Brazil are called Brazilians. Most Brazilians live in large cities. They speak Portuguese. It is Brazil's official language. Most Brazilians practice the Roman Catholic religion.

Families are important to Brazilians.
A Brazilian family enjoys a walk in the park.

Music is an important part of Brazil's culture. It is a mix of folk and modern sounds. Samba is the most popular style of music. It includes the sounds of tambourines, flutes, guitars, and *cuicas*. A *cuica* is a type of drum.

Musicians perform at Red Beach in Rio de Janeiro.

In the 1950s, samba and jazz music were blended together. They formed a new type of music called bossa nova. It is played on the piano, drums, guitar, and *berimbau*. The *berimbau* is a bow-shaped instrument with one string.

Dancing is a popular activity in Brazil. A special form of dance developed in Brazil. It is called *capoeira*. *Capoeira* is a mix of dance and **martial arts**. Music accompanies people who practice *capoeira*.

Carnival is an important celebration in Brazil. It takes place in the four days before Lent. Nearly 5 million people take part in Carnival in Brazil each year. It is a national holiday.

To celebrate Carnival, people attend parades, dance, and wear masks and costumes. Cities are decorated with lights and streamers. It is a party for the entire country.

Brazilians enjoy sports, too. Soccer is the most popular sport. Children play soccer in the streets. The country has professional soccer teams. Brazilians often observe the start and end of the World Cup.

Every year, 90,000 people watch the Carnival parade in Rio de Janeiro as it goes through a stadium nicknamed the Sambadromo.

The World Cup is the world's biggest soccer tournament. To celebrate, Brazilian fans paint city walls and streets. They hang yellow and green streamers, which are Brazil's team colors. Many workers take days off to watch the games.

Pickup games of soccer are part of daily life for many children in Brazil.

Brazilians celebrate Independence Day on September 7. It marks their freedom from Portugal. Brazilians watch parades, listen to concerts, and set off fireworks.

FUN FACT

ONE WORLD · MANY COUNTRIES

CHAPTER 5

DAILY LIFE

Daily life in Brazil often focuses on family.

Daily life in Brazil is mix of all the cultures that have created it. In the streets, musicians play drums to African rhythms. In homes, children recite nursery rhymes from Portugal. At meals, Brazilians may eat *açaí*, which is a berry native to the Amazon rain forest.

A favela is situated along a mountain near Rio di Janeiro.

Most Brazilians live in small apartments. High-rise apartment buildings are densely packed. Poor people live in *favelas* or shantytowns. Wealthy Brazilians live in large homes. Many native people live in huts in the rain forest.

Many Brazilians wear clothing similar to that worn in the United States. Jeans and T-shirts are popular. On the coast, beach clothing is common. People wear sandals, bathing suits, tank tops, shorts, or sundresses.

In the rain forest, native people wear little clothing. It is often just a small cloth tied around the waist. In other parts of

A man in the rain forest wears traditional clothing for a ritual ceremony.

Brazil, people wear traditional African clothing. Women wear bright colorful shawls, long full skirts, and head scarfs.

Brazilian food has many flavors. The national dish is *feijoada completa*. It is a mix of 20 dried, salted, or smoked meats. The meats simmer in a stew of black beans called *feijoadas*. It is served with rice and vegetables.

All-you-can-eat meat restaurants are also very popular in Brazil. The meats are soaked in a **marinade**. It adds flavor to the meat. Most meals include rice and beans. Salad and vegetables are side dishes.

A popular snack in Brazil is *agua de coco*. It is coconut water that is often sipped directly from a ripe coconut.

Fruits are part of most meals, too. Favorites are oranges, mangoes, pineapples, guava, and passion fruit. *Açaí* berries grow in Brazil on *açaí* palm trees. They are long, reddish-purple berries. They have become a popular health food around the world.

Another common food is *cassava*. It is a root vegetable similar to a potato. It can be eaten whole or ground into flour. Sometimes, Brazilians make fries with *cassava*.

Brazilian culture is a blend of modern and traditional. It is a country with a rich land and unique culture.

DAILY LIFE FOR CHILDREN

Children attend school in the morning or afternoon. Some classes have 40 students. They study the Portuguese language. They learn math, science, history, and geography.

After-school activities include sports. Children play soccer, volleyball, and table tennis. Competitions take place between schools.

For fun, children also play games. *Queimada* is tag played by two teams. Children stay active playing dodgeball, capture the flag, and tug-of-war. They jump rope. They play card games, marbles, and checkers, too.

Northern Brazil has many unique fruits. These include the sweet and tangy graviola, the sweet-and-sour bacuri, the cashew fruit cajú, and the tart acerola (above). These fruits flavor juice and ice cream.

FUN FACT

ONE WORLD · MANY COUNTRIES

FAST FACTS

Population: 202 million

Area: 3,287,612 square miles (8,514,877 sq km)

Capital: Brasília

Largest Cities: Brasília, Rio de Janeiro, and São Paulo

Form of Government: Federal Republic

Language: Portuguese

Trading Partners: China, the United States, and Argentina

Major Holidays: Carnival, Easter, and Independence Day

National Dish: *Feijoada* (a stew made with black beans and many kinds of meat)

Visitors to Rio de Janeiro can take a cable car ride to the top of Sugarloaf Mountain.

GLOSSARY

basin (BAY-suhn) A basin is an area of land that is drained by a river. The Amazon River has a large basin.

deforestation (de-for-uh-STAY-shun) Deforestation is the act of cutting down trees and other plants in a forest. Deforestation is a problem in the Amazon rain forest.

economy (ih-KON-uh-me) An economy is how a country runs its industry, trade, and finance. Brazil's economy is growing.

exported (EK-sported) Exported describes goods that have been sold to another country. Brazil has exported many goods.

livestock (LIVE-stahk) Livestock are animals raised on farms. Brazil's grassy plains are good for livestock.

marinade (MAIR-uh-nade) A marinade is a seasoned sauce in which meat, fish, or poultry are soaked. In Brazil, it is common to prepare meat using a marinade.

martial arts (MAR-shul ARTS) Martial arts are a practice that uses movements for self-defense or battle. Brazil's *capoeira* has movements from martial arts.

republic (ree-PUB-lick) A republic is a place where an elected official rules over the land and people. Brazil is a republic.

understory (UHN-duhr-stor-ee) An understory is a layer of plants that grow between the ground and the canopy of treetops. A rain forest has an understory.

To Learn More

BOOKS

Aloian, Molly. *The Amazon: River in a Rain Forest.* New York: Crabtree. 2010.

Ancona, George. *Capoeira: Game! Dance! Martial Art!* New York: Lee & Low Books, 2007.

Munduruku, Daniel. *Amazonia: Indigenous Tales from Brazil.* Toronto: Groundwood Books, 2013.

WEB SITES

Visit our Web site for links about Brazil: **childsworld.com/links**

Note to Parents, Teachers, and Librarians: We routinely verify our Web links to make sure they are safe and active sites. So encourage your readers to check them out!

Index